DUSTOFF
ENTER AT YOUR OWN RISK

Mike Disario

ISBN 978-1-63814-199-0 (Paperback)
ISBN 978-1-63814-209-6 (Hardcover)
ISBN 978-1-63814-208-9 (Digital)

Covenant Books, Inc.
11661 Hwy 707
Murrells Inlet, SC 29576
www.covenantbooks.com

This book is dedicated to Major Peter Dorland the DUSTOFF family: past, present, and future.

CONTENTS

FOREWORD

★ ⭐ ★

Anyone who understands and follows military history and military activities sooner or later learns about the word *DUSTOFF*. Throughout the years of military conflicts and war, the humane treatment and evacuation of the warriors—who are injured on the battlefield—are always a paramount part of the humanity of the battle.

During the Korean war in the early 1950s, the introduction of the helicopter on the battlefield was quick to show us—what a magnificent instrument it was for saving lives by providing a rapid and efficient evacuation mode for wounded soldiers.

The successful use of medical evacuation helicopters came of age during the Vietnam war of the 1960s. The efficient transport of seriously wounded soldiers from the forward combat battle to definitive medical treatment facilities was monumental. The radio call sign of DUSTOFF used by that helicopter crew became known by every infantryman as the battlefield angel that was going to carry you out of hell and, in a matter of minutes, transport you to a lifesaving field hospital.

The legend of DUSTOFF began in Vietnam, and its remarkable humanitarian story is still going strong today. This book reveals a part of that great legacy and is a compilation of a dozen evacuation missions as seen through the eyes of the flight medical crewman whose mission was to receive, stabilize, and keep alive the wounded patient during that short but critical flight from injury point to treatment facility.

The flight medic is the heart and soul of the battle-field—a helicopter angel that only owns the patient for a few short frantic minutes—but it is the flight medic that is the synergy of the reason, the power, and the wonder of that magnificent lifesaving team known by everyone around the world as DUSTOFF.

I had the privilege to serve and fly missions with the author of this book. This is the real stuff, folks, told by someone who lived it and felt firsthand the stress and emotions of each and every time the radio or bells called for a scramble to mission.

Only those warriors who have been in the arena of combat know the psychological feeling of comfort in the assurance that should you become wounded, the winged angel of DUSTOFF is but a moment away and a short flight to lifesaving help. Literally thousands of people are alive today because of the dedication and heroic efforts of these amazing helicopter teams.

It is my privilege to have been a small part of the great legend of DUSTOFF and my genuine honor to have soldiered with the author of this book. Sit back, grab a cup of coffee, buckle up, put your helmet on, and take an exciting ride on a few good missions.

Col. Ben Knisely
US Army, retired
DUSTOFF 65

CHAPTER 1

Edward's Air Force Base

Heading out for a rescue
mission at Edwards AFB.

Edward's Air Force Base (AFB) is a very famous place not just to the military aviation community, but to people everywhere. The base is a Mecca of great modern adventures in aviation. It's the place where Chuck Yeager first went faster than the speed of sound. It's the place where the space shuttle first flew and the place of countless other exciting and sometimes dangerous aviation firsts.

I will begin my story with my own meager involvement in that center of aviation firsts. I was employed as a flight medic for the US Army stationed at a remote desert base soon to be known as Fort Irwin, California. My job was a combination of emergency medical and technical rescue duties performed from a helicopter called a UH-1 or Huey, an old workhorse that had made a name for itself during the Vietnam War.

I was temporarily assigned to the army's test-flight center at nearby Edward's AFB, where the venerable Huey was used as a rescue helicopter to support the test flights that were performed on military airplanes and helicopters. I found myself standing on the hallowed vast expanse of tarmac, surrounded by dry lakebed as far as the eye could see. This assignment was the first in a long line of incredible adventures.

The rescue operation process came as quite a surprise to me. The basic idea was for the rescue helicopter to chase after and behind the test aircraft if it was a helicopter and to orbit outside the test area if it was an airplane. The rescue helicopter carried two big tanks of water and had a spray boom that projected from the front of the helicopter.

The crew consisted of a pilot and copilot, who occupied the cockpit, and a firefighter, who occupied the crew compartment in the rear of the helicopter. The firefighter wore a silver fire suit and had a box of specialized tools for ripping open a crashed aircraft. I was aboard as the flight medic. The medical equipment I carried included lots of burn bandages.

If an unlucky test pilot crashed, the rescue helicopter would fly over the pilot's aircraft and spray water on it in an attempt to put out the fire. The firefighter, in his silver fire suit, would get out and drag the injured aviator from the burning wreckage. If all went as planned, the survivor would be loaded onboard the rescue helicopter and be turned over to me. It was my job to keep the critically injured aviator alive until the helicopter could get to a medical facility.

The only fly in the ointment was that the medical facilities at Edward's AFB did not get the attention or funding that test programs received. Therefore, the injured test pilot had to be flown out of the high desert and into Los Angeles for medical treatment, which made my job even more interesting.

Let me tell you about two occasions when my morning helicopter ride got very exciting.

The first incident took place when a small US Air Force observer airplane crashed on the steep hillside of an Air Force bombing range. Because of strong winds that may have contributed to the crash, we could not reach the crash site until the following day. Upon landing on the hilltop, we scrambled down the rocky slope to the crash site.

The aircraft had crashed at a slow speed and burned on impact. This allowed the aircraft to melt around the dead pilot, leaving his burnt torso exposed from the waist up seemingly sitting upright in the burnt wreckage. His arms were burnt to stumps just past his elbows, and the wire frame of his headset was still sitting on his burnt cracked skull.

In an attempt to remove the pilot's remains, we grabbed him under each armpit and pulled him up and out of the burnt wreckage, resulting in the remains separating at the waist. We collected all the additional remains that we could and returned to the base.

The second incident involved an unfortunate two-man crew of an F-4 fighter plane. As this aircraft was streaking toward its intended target at low altitude, it hit the ground and the right wing was ripped off. The F-4 momentarily bounced back into the air and then started to roll. Immediately, both crew members ejected from the stricken aircraft. Because of the very low altitude and the spin of the F-4 after losing its wing, the ejection was only partly successful. Only the crew member in the back seat had enough time after ejection for his parachute to open before he hit the ground.

As our helicopter approached, we could see the burning remains of the aircraft and one crew member standing close to the crash site. Running toward the injured aviator, I yelled out to learn where the other crew member was. He pointed toward the burning wreckage.

I started to run in that direction but soon stopped. I could see the missing crew member's parachute, which was spread out unopened over the desert floor. The pilot in the front seat had not been as lucky as his counterpart in back but had hit the ground still in his ejection seat. The impact had thrown him across the desert floor to his death, his unopened parachute trailing behind.

We decided that since we had a doctor onboard, the helicopter would take the injured crew member back to the base for medical treatment. I would wait on-site with the dead pilot until an additional rescue helicopter arrived to collect the pilot's remains.

I realized, almost immediately, upon the helicopter's departure that I was alone in a desert valley full of unexploded bombs. I gave my attention to the F-4 that was burning no more than three hundred yards from me.

No sooner had the helicopter departed; the flaming wreckage began shooting off its highly explosive anti-tank rounds. The exploding rounds were flying all around the desert floor. I found a small boulder, the only cover around, and lay down flat behind it until the shooting stopped. I remember thinking, *Will this small boulder even stop an anti-tank round? When the rescue helicopter arrives, will it find two dead bodies?*

Shortly after the shooting had stopped, I heard the familiar sound of a helicopter off in the distance. As you can imagine, I was now a little tense. I took out my survival radio from my survival vest and tried to contact the incoming rescue helicopter. It was imperative that he land in a spot free of unexploded munitions. My survival radio was not working however, so I scrambled out from behind the boulder and resorted to the oldest and most reliable piece of survival gear I had—the survival mirror.

The helicopter, which was no more than a tiny dot in the sky five miles away, was flying a course parallel to my position and could not see the smoldering wreckage or me from that distance. It took three flashes of the survival mirror to get the helicopter to turn and fly directly toward me.

I searched around and found a spot that was safe and large enough to land the helicopter. However, the pilot decided not to follow my visual hand signals and instead set the helicopter down so close to a large unexploded round that the indentation of the helicopter skid tubed into the ground and caused the shell to actually shift position. I finished my morning at work by informing the hapless pilot that if it had not been for his seat harness, I would have pulled him entirely out of his helicopter and given him a firsthand look at his landing site.

CHAPTER 2

Fort Irwin

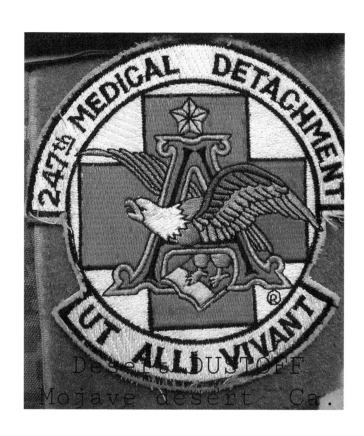

The famed entrance to
Ft. Irwin Ca.

Remembering that my tenure at Edward's AFB was only a temporary one, let's talk about the place where I worked full time.

Fort Irwin is located in the middle of the Mojave Desert in California, forty miles from the nearest town. The army purchased this vast desert area the size of Rhode Island from the California National Guard with the intention of training United States forces to fight a Soviet-style opponent in a realistic battle setting. The army wired the entire training area so they could record every mock battle in detail on videotape for later playback and analysis. The installation was newly opened when I arrived.

A single two-lane paved road leads to Fort Irwin. Part of that road stretches ten miles long, as straight as an arrow. It is preceded by a snaking curve that comes out of a pass and opens onto a dry lake bed. The winds can blow fierce across this lake bed and directly across the road as it curves out of the canyon. One of the first helicopter rescues (medevacs) flown at this installation was in response to a terrible car wreck reported on this curve. The following can only be described as an authentic miracle.

It didn't take the helicopter five minutes to arrive at the scene, and upon our approach, I could see items and metal strewn all over the crash site. On one side of the road, several cars had pulled over and people were milling around; on the other side of the road was a large pile of twisted metal. We landed close, and the crew chief—who was an onboard mechanic and medical assistant—and I rushed to the scene.

I discovered that the pile of twisted metal was the remains of a very large camper that fitted into the back of a large pickup truck. The pickup truck was sitting upright on the side of the road. Its cab and most of the truck's bed were as flat as a pancake. The crash caused the camper to completely open up, spreading its entire contents across the road and desert.

I hurried to the flattened pickup truck to, quite frankly, look for a body. Before I could get there, someone told me that the person sitting on the mattress across the road was the driver. I was amazed that anyone could have survived such a horrendous wreck.

I approached this unfortunate, yet lucky individual to see to his medical needs. I discovered that outside of a small cut on his nose resulting from the breaking of his glasses, he was miraculously unharmed. I also learned that this unfortunate individual was the new installation's first official Chaplain Fie who was arriving with all his worldly possessions in his pickup camper. This was to be his first day as chaplain to this new fort.

In recognition of the new training base, the army decided to have the biggest parachute drop since World War II. Five thousand paratroopers in approximately five hundred transport airplanes would fly all the way from the East Coast to the California desert. The objective was to perform a massive parachute drop on three dry lake beds located on the new installation.

In the way of medical preparation for this human rain, we had our own six helicopters and two we had borrowed, for a grand total of eight rescue helicopters. Each one was a UH1-V Medevac Huey with the capacity for two pilots, one crew chief, and one flight medic. Each one carried medical equipment and three litters. I won my first Army Commendation Medal for recommending that we put additional medical equipment onboard each helicopter and designate a staging area to rapidly replace supplies used in the potentially numerous rescues.

The day of the much-anticipated paradrop arrived. It was a beautiful morning as we flew out to the drop zone which consisted of three gigantic dry lake beds. A dry lake bed has the same consistency as a parking lot; in fact, the surface is so hard the military lands airplanes on them.

On the way to the drop zone, we spotted a ridge high on a cliff—a perfect perch from which to watch the unfolding drama below. We noticed, upon landing, that over twenty-one knots of wind were blowing across the drop zone. It is common knowledge that paratroopers are not dropped in winds that exceed twelve knots due to too much drifting of parachutes, as well as the potential for being dragged upon landing.

To cover the event, the army had invited Good Morning America, ABC, NBC, and CBS news to name the major media. All the media were located on a road between two of these dry lake beds.

An army captain had been assigned as the drop zone safety officer. His safety duties concerned wind speed and direction. He had the unfortunate task of informing the lieutenant general in the lead aircraft that the ground wind speed was between twenty-one and twenty-four knots, and that they were going to have to cancel the drop. The story was later told that the lieutenant general told the captain to find him twelve knots. This historic parachute drop would proceed as scheduled.

On this beautiful, clear desert morning, we sat in our helicopter, watching the sun rise in the east; and as it rose, we could see the airplanes arriving from a distance. It was an amazing sight. Giant transport aircraft looking like little dots grew bigger and bigger. There were hundreds of them flying in formation below us between the two ridges that bordered the drop zone.

We knew, however, that between those two ridges, the wind speed exceeded twelve knots and that they were not going to drop five thousand paratroopers in such conditions. We were a little disappointed thinking that the drop would be called off. We could not hear the captain on the ground talking to the lieutenant general because they were on a different radio frequency, and so we did not know that the drop was still going to proceed.

The first series of aircraft came through the valley off to one side of the central drop zone and dropped what is called the heavy drop. This consisted of the big earthmovers and other large engineering equipment that are utilized in an airborne assault. We figured they had decided to proceed only with the heavy drop. As the remaining aircraft took their turns over the drop zone, however, paratroopers started jumping out of the airplanes.

Paratroopers usually fall almost horizontally when coming out of the aircraft doors; when the chutes open, the paratroopers fall vertically. On this day, the paratroopers continued falling horizontally even after their parachutes had opened. The paratroopers rocketed into the parking-lot hard, dry lake beds sideways and were dragged rapidly because of the wind.

There was a dead silence in our aircraft for about three minutes, which seemed like an hour. Then all at once, the silence was broken with the voices of frightened and angry paratroopers screaming into their field radios the words, "DUSTOFF! Medevac! Lifesaver!"

Even before the first wave of cries for help had died down, we were airborne from our cliff perch and were diving into the valley below. The situation immediately went from bad to worse. Because of the large numbers of parachutes, paratroopers (injured or not) and related equipment spread about the vast drop zone—the scene below us was in confusion.

The eight rescue helicopters could see what was developing on the ground, but the paratroopers below could only see the medevac aircraft circling above. The immediate insurmountable problem was how to get eight helicopters, with their whirling blades, into a valley filled with military men and equipment; find and land next to an injured person; and then take off safely after loading the injured paratrooper.

As the pilots in the helicopters talked among themselves about how to best coordinate a controlled rescue, the calls from below stated pleadingly that they could see a medevac helicopter overhead. This did not help the pilots pinpoint a specific target among the mass of military men and equipment below.

A perfect example of this occurred almost immediately. One desperate paratrooper yelled over his radio, "DUSTOFF, I see you. Turn left now!" As you can imagine, all the helicopter pilots were eager to respond to the first direct call that was issued. Every helicopter turned left which, from the ground, made it look as though a helicopter was finally arriving; but then a helicopter would suddenly turn away because someone else just told it to turn left.

One of the paratroopers on the ground who was standing over a dying friend became tired of waiting for a helicopter to spot him. He took the initiative and announced into his radio that he was going to "pop smoke." This meant he was going to ignite a smoke grenade to mark his position on the ground so he could be seen from the air better.

One of the pilots—hearing the desperation in the paratrooper's voice—said, more to calm him than anything else, "Go ahead, pop smoke." From my position over the drop zone, I could see the smoke begin to stream downwind from the spot where it was ignited. Well I thought, in my ignorance, that was easy; damn good thing he had smoke.

No sooner had I finished this thought that it became terribly apparent that every paratrooper standing over an injured or dead comrade also saw the immediate effectiveness of this signaling. Soon the entire valley was filled with the smoke of a hundred smoke grenades. The only blessing was the wind that quickly dissipated the smoke.

Because of our position, we were able to swoop in on one of the first smokes that went off. Our first stop was for a lieutenant who had been dragged across the lake bed so severely that his face was unrecognizable. He looked as if he had two right arms because his back was broken so badly. I cared for this person as best as I could, and we loaded him onto the helicopter. The pilot, who also was my unit's commander, informed me that we were not going back to the hospital until we had filled all three litters.

As this tragedy unfolded over and over all morning, I was reduced to hoping that the next time we returned to the drop zone, the first injured soldier we picked up would not be one who was dying.

This incredulous event went on until all 126 injured and thirteen dead had been evacuated from the drop zone. Simply by chance, the California National Guard had an army field hospital in training at Fort Irwin at the time.

Besides the small hospital on the installation, this welcomed asset gave us an additional site to deliver the casualties. I also transported nine soldiers with critical head injuries from the base to a medical center in San Bernardino, California.

I hope that you are beginning to understand the world of DUSTOFF. I must state here, however, that unlike all other army helicopter units, a medevac helicopter goes out on its missions alone. This is unique to military aviation. In all other military helicopter missions, the workload is shared by launching two or more aircraft to complete a given mission.

CHAPTER 3

Night Missions

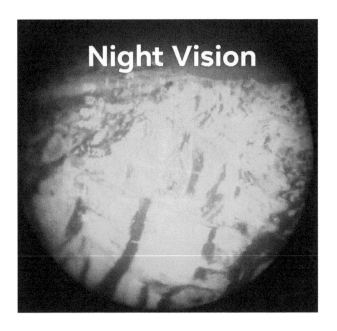

So far I have introduced you to the daylight world of medevac. But to understand the real intensity of the mission as it evolves, one must experience the night. One of the facts of nature about a vast desert is that at night, with no artificial light anywhere on the horizon, it can be virtually pitch-black in all directions—including up and down. Before there were night-vision devices, we navigated using the light of a good moon and by following roads. We resorted to a spotlight, a map, and a lot of memory when conditions were worse. This regularly was, in itself, a terrifying experience—especially when landing.

As a helicopter approaches the ground for landing, the rotating blades kick up an immense cloud of dust. This condition requires the pilot to land quickly before the dust cloud reduces outside visibility to the point where the pilot can no longer see the ground. This maneuver is an art that is difficult during the day.

At night, it becomes a matter of skill and luck. From a personal standpoint, landing successfully, becomes a distant second to your patient's potential life-threatening injuries in the immediate priority list of night-rescue missions.

To illustrate the remote darkness that one confronts in the desert at night, I will tell you a short story about flying at night in the desert.

We had been flying rescue missions for several months on this huge training installation that was to be the crown jewel of the army's new high-tech training doctrine. Before the official opening, an entourage of high-ranking military officers from the Pentagon requested an air tour of the new training area.

It was decided that since the medevac folks knew the training area best, they would have the honor of flying these dignitaries around. My commander suggested that the dignitaries' meeting with the general be cut short in order to afford enough daylight for viewing the installation. However, the general's staff curtly informed my commander that the general had the utmost confidence in his medevac pilot's ability to fly the dignitaries whenever they arrived for their flight. My commander, being a good soldier, saluted and left.

The entourage arrived for their flight approximately one hour before dark. Without comment we seated them and took off to the east. It was dark before we left the main installation. My commander gleefully commenced with a running monologue about the invisible landmarks below us as we flew in the pitch dark.

After the appropriate amount of shocked silence by our welcomed guests, we were humbly asked to carefully return our precious cargo to the safe confines of the lighted installation. All future requests for tours were presented with a morning takeoff time.

Once night-vision devices arrived to aid us in our mission, the night mission terror factor actually went way up for the crew members in the back of the helicopter. Before, it had taken the entire crew to navigate at night, using a spotlight and a signal light from the people on the ground. So we were all scared together, frantically trying to see all around us.

The early model night-vision devices were only issued to the pilots up-front, which was a dramatic improvement to their ability to fly at night. However, the devices required that no ambient light be on in the helicopter. This left the two crew members in the back sitting in complete blackness flying over a hundred miles an hour through desert canyons in the middle of nowhere in the dead of night. The only sight to be seen from the back of the helicopter was the rhythmic flash of a canyon wall as it was illuminated for a split second when our aircraft position light flashed.

I always internally greeted the announcement that we were preparing to land with a fatalistic trust. In afterthought, I suppose it was a built-in defense mechanism designed to prevent me from becoming totally involved in my fate upon landing so that I could focus on my mental exercise of imagining the innumerable possible medical scenarios that might momentarily be thrust in my face.

I bring this point up now to illustrate a fact of life in the emergency medical profession. As anyone who has had any involvement at all with emergency response can tell you, the accuracy of the information given from the scene at the time of the crisis is usually the most unreliable factor in a medevac mission. I learned early on that the reason we were flying to an emergency in the middle of the night was because the medical people on the ground had run out of answers.

That being the case, coupled with the possibility of inaccurate information regarding the patient's medical condition, I discovered that the best way to handle night missions (and all missions in general) was to focus on inbound radio updates of the patient's condition while running over possible scenarios in my mind. That seemed to be the most effective way to not think about the murderous blackness outside my little helicopter.

As a helicopter starts to land, the noises and vibrations take on a special pitch. That pitch starts the "pucker factor," a dramatic increase in anxiety. The next thing that indicates which direction the pucker factor will go is the amount of chatter from the pilots up-front. The final variable affecting the pucker factor is that a helicopter cannot land straight down in the desert. If it attempts to land straight down, it will blow up too much sand and "brown-out." This means the pilots will not be able to see down during the critical last few feet. This condition has led to innumerable desert helicopter crashes.

After the helicopter finally bumped to a stop, it was time for me to open my door and step out, looking like the hero with all the answers. Regardless of whether I could see anyone or not (and usually I couldn't), with luck, the pilots would have told me which direction into the darkness we should boldly run. And off we would boldly go, hoping to bump into someone—me with my medical-aid bag over my shoulder, and my crew chief in tow with all the additional medical equipment

Sure enough, we never went too far before someone grabbed us and dragged us into the awaiting pandemonium. On numerous occasions, the awaiting individuals were so out of answers that they did not wait for us to come to them. These occasions were by far the worst. After the harrows of flying to the site of the medical emergency, being able to momentarily get away from the helicopter and take a breather while assessing the situation would have been a welcome respite.

When outside a helicopter, the place not to be is near it—meaning under or around the blades. After opening the door and stepping out into the darkness, the worst thing you can see is a group of scared soldiers running at you with one or more bodies bouncing up and down on litters. The reason for this is twofold. First, the more people that you have running around your helicopter in the dark in a semi-panicked state, the more likely it is you will end up with more patients and possibly no ride home. Second, this usually means that the body being bounced up and down is almost dead.

After working as fast as I possibly could to board my patient(s) on the helicopter, the only remaining task was to keep them alive in the crowded back compartment of a pitch-dark, low, and fast flying helicopter. The positive aspect of that part of the mission was that I usually was way too busy to worry about running into something (including the ground) on the way back to the medical facility.

Remember that the pilots flying this helicopter were using their night-vision devices and that this required the interior of the helicopter to be as dark as possible. Even the instrument lights in the cockpit were modified to emit a very dim red light that would not adversely affect a pilot's vision under the night-vision devices.

Since the helicopter's interior is open between the cockpit (front) and the crew area (back), those of us in the back were forced to utilize small lights with red filters on them to examine and treat our patients. We also employed these lights to find, utilize, and keep track of all the medical equipment as well as to keep medical notes and talk on the radio to the receiving medical facility.

In adjusting to this environment, the one factor that couldn't be overcome was the fact that under dim red light at night, it was impossible to distinguish between moisture and blood. Many times I waited to see if the fluid turned sticky, an indicator of drying blood. Always it was a surprise when I finally got my patients under the bright lights in the emergency department.

While the helicopter pilots were blessed with this new technology, the soldiers on the ground were not as lucky. For this reason, they responded to the sound of a rescue helicopter in the traditional way—which was to try and make radio contact with the helicopter.

Whether or not contact was made, the next step was to make sure the helicopter could see them. In a vast, dark desert, the best way to get noticed is to use the brightest light available. The unfortunate drawback to night-vision devices is that if they are exposed to bright light conditions while operating, they automatically shut down. This has the effect of instantaneously blinding both pilots.

On one particular mission, the worst happened as we approached the landing site in a very tight and steep box canyon. Although the pilots had contacted the individuals on the ground and told them that the helicopter would be landing "blacked out," meaning with the use of night-vision equipment, the message not to turn on any lights didn't reach the people in a tank next to the landing site.

Upon realizing that the rescue helicopter was going to land near it, the tank waited until the helicopter was just above the landing site to turn on its spotlight to help the helicopter see the right spot. Just like that, the pilots were now blind.

Once a helicopter starts to land, it is difficult to abort the landing. It requires coordinated maneuvers to regain lift and air speed. Seeing where you are going also is essential. The crew members in the back were still in the dark, except for the tank's bright light, and we were flying in a box canyon. As the pilots ripped off their night-vision devices and started a climbing turn to the left (my side), for just a split second during the last position, I could see a light flash out my side of the helicopter that we didn't have a lot of space on my side between the canyon wall and the helicopter.

As we turned toward the wall, I could feel—up and down my spine—the wall getting closer. As we completed the turn, the alarm in my head had already gone off, screaming at me that there was no physical way we could make the turn without hitting the canyon wall. As we completed the turn and the feeling in my spine dissipated, I realized that was the closest thing that I had seen to a miracle. All that remained was to let the pilots stop screaming at the poor guys on the ground about the idiot in the tank, land the helicopter, and let the medic go to work.

Fortunately, it didn't take the system long to get us poor folks in the back of the helicopter night-vision devices as well. The obvious military logic had nothing to do with relieving our rides of terror but with providing the pilots two more sets of eyes. The guys in the back had, on occasion, been allowed to glimpse the night as the pilots knew it. Now we were all equipped to view the green light of an artificially bright night.

As with all inventions, our new vision was both a blessing and a curse. I could not only see where I was going but, more importantly, could help with clearing the flight of the helicopter and with the all-important landing. With night-vision devices on, however, the world appeared green, and there was almost no distance or depth perspective. The range of view has been best described as "looking through a pair of toilet paper tubes." You had to constantly move your head to scan the horizon. Those early devices were bulky, modified affairs that required a counterweight mounted to the back of the helmet to balance the weight of the device on the front.

Having night vision shifted the emotions of the mission to a point where it was fun to be able to run past the semi-panicked soldiers stumbling around in the darkness. It was a blessing to be able to go directly to my patients and see my way back to the helicopter. However, the devices were designed for vision past eighteen inches. Patient care is done in the back of a helicopter at closer than 18 inches because of cramped space. This made the devices useless for patient care, and on the way to the hospital, it was back to the old-fashioned dark red world. Bright-green world with no depth perception and "toilet-paper-tube" perspective on the way out and dark red world on the way back. By the way, in both worlds, blood is just another background colored fluid.

Occasionally, *trauma* takes on a different meaning from the usual physical form that one has become adjusted to dealing with. In the following case, the trauma had its root in irony.

A young mother married to a soldier stationed at Fort Irwin had given birth to a child who had died of Sudden Infant Death Syndrome (SIDS) within a month or two after birth. The young mother apparently had a foreboding about her new child that had been chalked up to postpartum depression.

The overwhelming sense of foreboding regarding her newborn had strained her to the breaking point. When her fears were realized, she fell apart and had to be transferred to a major military medical center with psychiatric care services. The task fell to me to transfer her by helicopter to San Diego to a naval hospital. I spent the two-hour flight caught between silence and comforting words.

About a year later, another mission came down for a transfer to San Diego with a psychiatric patient. As an initial step in the transfer procedure, I went over to the hospital to be briefed as to my patient's status. I was told that the patient was a young wife who had recently given birth to a child and had convinced herself that the child was going to die of SIDS.

Before I even saw the patient, I knew instinctively who it was. It seemed that immediately after the birth of her second child, this poor woman again had the same feelings of foreboding. She was convinced that the death of her first child was due to her physical separation from the child during the night. Confronted with the fear of separation leading to the death of her baby, the young mother would not even sleep. Eventually this paranoid vigilance caused the young woman to collapse from lack of sleep and from being a nervous wreck.

The woman's husband had no choice, but to bring her to the hospital, where it was decided she would be transferred to the same San Diego military hospital she had been taken to the first time. She pleaded with her husband and the doctors not to separate her from her baby. She was convinced that it would lead to the baby's death. She was so excited and adamant that the physicians decided to sedate and restrain her for the trip. Thankfully this made my trip with this patient less difficult than the first trip.

That evening, the grateful husband and father went to bed for a good night's sleep, turned on the new SIDS alarm, fell into a deep sleep, and never heard the SIDS alarm go off.

CHAPTER 4

Fort Drum

The medevac program at Fort Drum was unique for several reasons. Primarily, though, it was used by the army to sell to the civilian populace of upstate New York the idea of having a major military installation in their backyard.

Former President Richard Nixon founded the Military Assistance to Safety and Traffic (MAST) program after the Vietnam War. Its purpose was to utilize the highly trained medevac helicopter crews returning from the war as a government assistance program to local, state, and federal rescue authorities. The program was practically cost free to the involved community. Their incurred cost was only for specific equipment and training.

The idea was that communities that hosted a military installation with a medevac unit asset would have emergency medical support by a military medevac helicopter with no incurred liability or financial commitment. Despite the obvious benefits of this new emergency medical capability, our unit (at the behest of the new army fort) had to spend almost six months selling our free service to the established emergency medical service (EMS) providers, who were mostly volunteers. The military establishment at Fort Drum spared no expense in allowing us to utilize our helicopters for the purpose of public relations.

In that initial six-month "honeymoon," we flew to almost every fire hall and rescue service that we could reach by air. I was even encouraged to write an article for the regional EMS news, stating the case for calling the new medevac service as opposed to transporting patients by ground ambulance.

In conjunction with the new emergency medical resource, one of the two local hospitals invested in a brand-new state-of-the-art helipad to be built on the hospital roof. This new addition brought significant local media coverage. From the dedication to the first few practice landings by our helicopters, the local news coverage grew. The almost nightly news updates on the progress of the exciting MAST program made us quite popular indeed.

As we practiced our procedures for utilizing the new hospital helipad under the glow of the news cameras, the city firemen who were required to respond each and every time we landed or took off from the helipad could be seen in the background. This requirement led the city fire chief to see a need to add new resources and capital to his beloved department.

The fire chief, in this case, also was the city fire marshal—meaning he had the sole authority in the city to determine the fire codes. In this case, the "fireman of many hats" decided that for the hospital helipad to operate legally in the city, it would require an increase in the budget of the city fire department. Until that time, the new hospital helipad was closed by order of the city fire marshal.

Before the new helipad was built, the system for delivering a patient to the hospital by helicopter was to land on the outskirts of the city in a school sports field and transfer the patient to an awaiting ambulance. The transition from helicopter to ambulance and then to the hospital added an additional ten minutes, at a minimum, to the transfer time. In an environment where seconds count, the new hospital helipad would be a lifesaver.

As you can imagine, the local press—great fans of the new helipad as well as the new medevac program—wasted no time in publicizing the new dilemma concerning the fire chief's controversial decision. The published position of the fire chief was that his current budget could not support the additional fire response requirements of the new hospital helipad.

The position of the hospital was that they had installed fire-fighting equipment on the helipad. Experts on helicopter-aviation safety were brought in to testify that, historically, helicopters do not crash on the helipad but traditionally crash during landing or takeoff. This was intended to show that if a helicopter *should*, crash it would do so not on the roof but somewhere else. Unfortunately, this only further isolated and hardened the fire chief's position. The result was a one-sided polarization of the community.

During this period of strained relations between the city fathers and the fire chief, the medevac program continued to flourish and be recognized by the community as a positive thing. However, we still had to land outside the city and transfer our patients to awaiting ambulances for the final journey to the hospital emergency room and the lifesaving care their injuries required. Well, true to form, I would be thrust into this fray whether I liked it or not.

On a dark December night, shortly before Christmas, the call came in for a MAST mission. I had the honor that evening of being the flight medic on duty. The request to respond came from the scene of an accident on a rural stretch of a two-lane highway. Soon after our departure from the airfield, the details of the scene started coming in to us by radio from the emergency crews already present at the scene. They stated that the accident involved a compact car and a logging truck. There was one critically injured, entrapped victim.

Upon arriving at the scene, it immediately became obvious this was one of those rare occasions when the report of the accident was not worse than the actual accident itself. As I left the noise and wind of the helicopter and stepped into the night past our landing light, I headed toward the concentration of emergency lights on the nearby roadway.

I was greeted, as usual, by a group of emergency responders of all types as they shouted their personal interpretations of the scene at me in unison. I did what I always do when confronted by the ever-present mob of helpers: I looked where I was going, summed up the scene, and listened to the key words of the individual deemed most knowledgeable about the events unfolding.

As I came into the lights, I could see that the situation was uniquely bad. It appeared that the logging truck had been attempting a three-point turn for the purpose of backing into a farm track off the main road. A compact car traveling down the road did not see the truck spanning the road. The impact of the car into the side of the large logging truck caused the top of the car to collapse and become wedged under the logging truck.

The compact car had a rear hatchback that provided the only access to the patient. After crawling into the car through the destroyed hatchback, I could see that the patient was a young woman with a very bad head injury. Because of the seriousness of her condition, it was imperative to get her out of the car and to a hospital as soon as possible.

As I tried to give her the best medical care that I could, the rescue crews at the scene were frantically trying to free the car from under the logging truck. First they flattened the tires of the car to add a little space. Then they tried to jack-up the side of the logging truck that the car was wedged under. Precious time was ticking away, and the car was still stuck under the logging truck.

In an act of what can only be described as desperation, the decision was made to attach a steel cable from a tow truck to the back bumper of the car. I was not consulted during the decision-making because I was busy with the patient. I was changing the patient's oxygen bottles while a cable was being attached to the bumper of the car, and I wasn't aware of what was transpiring until I felt the tension being applied to the car.

The roof of the car was crushed down so far that to access the patient, I had positioned myself so that I was kneeling in the trunk area and bending forward over the patient's right shoulder. This left my butt and legs sticking up and out of the hatchback area. By the time I realized what was about to happen, I could do no more than tense up and wait for the inevitable snap and whoosh of flying steel cable.

Right on cue, the cable snapped, and I waited that split second for the searing pain. Luckily for me, the cable snapped at my end. As the deadly snake recoiled back toward the wrecker, it passed by numerous emergency workers, each of whom were thinking what had just gone through my mind. The hapless wrecker driver and his assistants, in this botched attempt, had only to bear the brunt of a state policeman's reminder of their stupidity.

Eventually, more professional heads prevailed. After the firemen and their "jaws of life" were through with the car, we managed to get the patient out of the wreckage. At that time, I was better able to assess and treat the patient's injuries. As rapidly as possible, we loaded her and all the related medical equipment required to keep her alive onto the helicopter and took off into the night. My assessment revealed that the patient was truly in critical condition from a massive head injury. Her bodily systems were starting to shut down due to the extensive trauma to her head.

As we flew toward the city, I informed my pilot of the seriousness of our patient's condition. I stated that in this case, the patient might not survive the additional time it would take to transfer her to an awaiting ambulance out-side the city and then on to the hospital according to nor-mal procedure. Because it was common knowledge that the helipad was legally closed, an on-the-spot decision had to be made by the pilot.

The pilot on duty that night was an old veteran who trusted his flight medic and made decisions confidently. It didn't take him long to reach the hospital on the radio and advise them that we were inbound to their rooftop helipad with a patient with a critical head injury. After a moment of shocked silence from the emergency room staff, the emergency department acknowledged our transmission and very hesitantly reminded us that the helipad was, in fact, legally closed.

The pilot glanced over his shoulder at the patient and then at me. His look said, *Should we go for it?* I had already decided that it was necessary to be in the emergency room as fast as possible. I had sent up a silent cheer when the pilot stated his intent to the hospital. Now as I returned his glance, I left no doubt as to my approval of his intentions. The pilot acknowledged the information sent from the hospital and reiterated his intent as matter-of-factly as possible.

It must be said here that the conversation between the pilot and the hospital was by no means private. As with most civilian emergency system radio frequencies, everyone with a scanner or a radio could easily monitor all transmissions by radios on that frequency. Considering the publicity surrounding the helipad affair, the entire region was now aware of what was transpiring at the hospital roof helipad.

Being only too aware of the commotion our act would cause, the pilot decided that immediately after delivering the patient and myself at the rooftop helipad, he would depart with the helicopter and the remaining crew and go directly to the landing zone outside the city. I would accompany my patient to the emergency room and give a more definitive description of the patient's injuries and the treatments administered so far. I would then catch a ride with an ambulance or a police car out to the landing zone to rejoin my crew.

As the helicopter made its final approach to the rooftop helipad, we could see the police and fire trucks gathered below. My attention immediately shifted to the awaiting hospital staff on the roof as soon as we touched down. The procedure for unloading patients had been practiced with much fanfare and publicity. Now as I looked out my door,

I could see that the faces waiting for us were the same, but the expressions on the faces were uniformly different than before. The expressions said, *This is for real, and not only that: this means trouble.*

Regardless of the consequences, training took over and we unloaded the patient off the helicopter and brought her to the emergency room. After the initial few minutes in the emergency room, the pace slackened as the emergency room staff took over the patient's care. As people started to approach me, the reality of our illegal act emerged. I must confess that a sort of rebel-celebrity status immediately started to take hold.

Before I had even left the emergency room, my mood had turned to indignation and anger upon being informed that my crew was under arrest at the behest of the fire chief. The charges were something like flagrant violation of a city fire code, public endangerment, causing the fire chief to respond to the scene of a violation in his pajamas, etc.

The official and public response to this was immediate. The commanding general of Fort Drum informed the local community that MAST was closed to the public until such time as we were again welcome. Telegrams and letters arrived from everyone from firemen to senators. Much to my relief, it did not take the good people of northern New York long to straighten out this unfortunate affair and clear us to utilize the helipad from then on.

A footnote to this bizarre story concerns the patient's critical head injury, which consisted of a large indentation to the right-rear side of her head. In every car accident I had previously attended, the driver's head injuries always occurred either to the front or the left side of the head. How in the world did this patient manage to crush the right rear of her head?

Later, as the sun rose over the accident scene and the emergency crews were still cleaning up the wreckage, a state policeman driving to the scene saw something lying in the roadside ditch about a hundred yards from the wreck. When he stopped to examine it, he was surprised to see that it was a brand-new bowling ball. As he picked it up, he noticed some blood and hair on it.

Apparently the bowling ball had just been purchased as a Christmas present for a loving husband. It was being transported home in the back of a hatchback car that night. The impact with the side of the logging truck had sent the bowling ball rocketing from the back of the car. As it continued to travel forward after the impact, the bowling ball struck the patient in the right rear of her head, went through the windshield, and on down the road into the darkness.

huey rescue
helicopters in
Germany.

Sling loading an
entire emergency
room

Ready for work in the Blackhawk.

brand new Blackhawks on display.

usns mercy
Persian gulf
desert storm

Official patches for USNS Mercy during Desert Storm

Our hero during Desert Storm

In front of our headquarters in Bahrain Shield/Storm

CHAPTER 5

Germany

blackhawk in Germany.

My next stop in this global journey was Germany. I found myself on a hilltop outside the city of Stuttgart. My unit's mission was to provide all the helicopter rescues performed by the army throughout Europe, but primarily in Germany at that time. Upon my arrival, the unit was still using the venerable UH-1 helicopters. Within the first six months of my arrival, however, the unit was selected to receive the brand new UH-60 Blackhawk helicopter.

These bigger, faster, and certainly more advanced helicopters were a lifesaver in more ways than one. In the initial days of the transition to the new helicopter, there was much partisan discussion about which helicopter was better. I personally had decided that the new helicopter had advantages in interior room (my personal prerequisite), range and speed of flight, and ability to fly in certain weather conditions. These advantages were possible because of all the instrumentation and equipment that the new helicopter came equipped with.

The new helicopter had such remarkable devices such as instruments that calculated the helicopter's height above the ground and a computerized positioning system (Doppler) that tracked the helicopter's position in the air relative to its position above the ground. Another new innovation was the helicopter's ability to fly in weather conditions where icing was predicted, meaning that ice would build up on the rotor blades and prohibit the helicopter from flying. Special heating elements had been added to the rotor blades to prevent ice from forming.

Like all new aircrafts, the technological advances of the new UH-60 did not have all the bugs worked out of them. The venerable old Huey, on the other hand, had all the bugs worked out of it long ago. It was simpler to fly and maintain, and it was constructed entirely of metal. The new high-tech helicopter was made from all kinds of material—including metal, plastic, and Kevlar.

I will now describe the events that made me a believer in the new technology. Our crew of four was heading back to base with a doctor who had accompanied the patient we had just dropped off at a military hospital. The trip to the hospital had been uneventful. We had picked up the patient from one military hospital and delivered him to another. We had flown the distance in between at a higher altitude and in the clouds, using the instruments for navigation at seven thousand feet above sea level (*sea level* being the standard setting for all height indicators in aircraft that can fly in the clouds). Our course back home took us directly over the mountains; at some points, the mountains were 2,500 feet higher than sea level.

Everybody was relaxed as we flew back in the clouds, and I began to doze off since there was nothing to see outside the window. Suddenly, the loudest bang and flash I had ever heard or seen occurred. The helicopter immediately started to shake to a point where I had to hang on to my seat and couldn't focus on anything. The aircraft started to fall out of the sky. The rotor blades were still turning, but the shaking was intense.

At first, the pilot thought that one of the deicing elements inside one of the main rotor blades had blown up, causing the blade to blow up. The copilot believed an engine had blown up. The instruments were useless at this point. All instrumentation was either shut off or was giving false indications. Every light on the emergency failure panel had lit up, indicating failures in every aircraft system.

The pilot was able to control the aircraft with great difficulty, and he was in a left descending turn that he couldn't do much about. The best he could do was to keep the helicopter level. Both engines seemed to be running, but there was no electronic control to them anymore. The copilot had to lock the engines out of their automatic-operation mode and manually control both engines using the two throttle controls. It was critical to keep the engines from going too slow or too fast, and it was equally important to keep the engines turning at the same speed. All of this was accomplished in a matter of seconds under shaking and vibrations that were just incredible.

Just as the reality of our predicament was hitting us, the next fearful acknowledgment was that we were falling through the clouds. The helicopter broke below the clouds around 3,500 feet above the ground, which gave us about a thousand feet before we reached the level of the mountain-tops. As we were falling out of the sky, the helicopter was stuck in a descending left-hand turn.

Looking down, we could see that the left turn was taking us right down the side of a mountain and into a large field between two mountains. If we had descended below the clouds on the opposite side of the mountain, we would have smashed right into its side.

The helicopter hit the ground in a level attitude. The impact was hard enough to bury the landing gear all the way up to the aircraft's belly. Miraculously, no one was injured; in fact, everybody walked away from the crash site. The damage to the helicopter was extensive. One of the helicopter tail rotor blades was completely blown away. The end of one of the main rotor blades also was blown off. All of the plastic in the bearings that controlled the rotor blades, and therefore the flight of the helicopter, were burnt away. The entire electronics system was destroyed.

We managed to send a brief distress call, "Mayday, on the way down," but due to our rapid descent and the mountainous terrain, we had no idea if it had been heard. Immediately after the shaking rotor blades of the helicopter stopped their death dance outside my window, I got the hell out of there.

After several minutes of standing with my mouth open, staring at what was left of our brand-new helicopter, the training kicked in and I pulled out my survival radio from my survival vest. Turning it on, I tried to contact someone on the emergency channel. After a moment of static, the voice of a pilot in a rescue helicopter came over my radio, asking if we could see or hear his helicopter.

No sooner had he asked then, I heard off in the distance that old familiar sound—the sound of a venerable old Huey coming to the rescue. Even though I had just decided that the new UH-60 was the best at rescue jobs, not to mention that it had just saved my life, I had to admit that nothing sounded better than the noise of an old Huey in the distance, getting closer as it came to the rescue.

The final determination was that our helicopter had been hit by lightning, the first Blackhawk ever to be so honored. The lightning had struck one of the main rotor blades about three feet from the hub where all the blades come together. The lightning bolt left a huge black mark that looked like a gigantic spot weld. The bolt apparently traveled down to the rotor shaft; traveled through the engines and transmission; passed down the tail; and exited out the tail rotor, blowing off one rotor blade.

I became an immediate and total convert to the new helicopter after the true extent of its damages was assessed. Having spent a lot of time in the older UH-1 helicopter—and having seen the results of other crashes I was involved in—I was convinced that under the same circumstances, there would have been a much darker outcome for the UH-1.

Sikorsky Aircraft Corporation, which built the helicopter, actually bought the damaged aircraft back from the army to perform studies and tests to determine what damage occurred from the lighting strike.

The two pilots who managed within a couple of seconds to assess the situation and work together to save our collective asses both got the US Army's prestigious Broken Wing Award. This award is given to pilots who, despite overwhelming odds, manage to get their *very* broken aircraft down in one piece.

One advantage of an assignment in a foreign country is the chance to work with members of the military of other nations. Shortly after receiving the new Blackhawk helicopters, an act of terrorism occurred against Americans in Germany, and the possibility of a threat to the new helicopters was now perceived as more real.

It happened that a request came in for a helicopter rescue in the middle of the night. The mission was to fly to a remote location to pick up a soldier with possible appendicitis. The location of the request was not a usual or familiar one to us, and because of this, it took us additional time to arrive there. We had intermittent radio contact with the people on the ground on the way to the site.

Finally, a light appeared out of the darkness, illuminating a spot on the top off a hill and in a field. As we descended within three hundred feet off the ground, the light that was guiding us went out. We continued the descent a little further, but since we were not certain how flat the landing zone was, the decision was made to circle and try again.

Once more, at about three hundred feet, the guiding light was extinguished. We circled again, but this time we had a better view of the landing zone from our last approach. On this approach to land, the guiding light stayed on until we were just above the ground; but by then, our own landing light had illuminated the area enough so that we did not require any additional light.

There was a little slope to the landing site that caused my side of the helicopter to settle lower than the other side. The grass was knee-high in the field, which made it as tall as the bottom of the helicopter. The helicopter-landing light was dimmed and defused by the grass so that the normal distance around the helicopter couldn't be seen. Normally the area illuminated outside the helicopter is as large as the diameter of the rotor blades. Due to the high grass, however, the ring of light practically stopped under the helicopter.

No one approached us after we landed. I opened my door, and the crew chief opened his door so we could locate someone in the darkness. Just as I was stepping out of the helicopter, I noticed that the pilot on my side was looking and pointing. I looked in the same direction and saw someone moving toward the aircraft in the darkness. Because of the darkness around the helicopter, we could not see the individual until he was already under the turning rotor blades.

As I stepped out of the helicopter, I saw running into the light a man with long brown hair dressed in a sweater and civilian clothes and carrying an AK-47, a Russian/Eastern Bloc assault rifle. Well this was totally unprecedented. Upon seeing this most alarming event unfold next to his helicopter, the pilot took the flight controls and shouted at me, "Get in, get in!" We both assumed at the same instance that this was an act of terrorism in progress.

I backed up to jump into the helicopter. Just as I jumped and got my butt in the doorway, I saw that this guy was already at the side of the helicopter and moving toward the front. The pilot was yelling, "Get in, get in, we have to get out of here!"

When the man with the AK-47 saw that the pilot was yelling for me to get in, he turned toward me and I hit him right on the nose. I was so scared. I hit him right on the nose with the palm of my hand, pushing him real hard. He fell over backward, and we were up and out of there.

As we were leaving in a great hurry, the requesting unit finally broke radio silence. The voice on the other end of the radio was that of an American soldier. He asked us to please return, stating that he still had an injured man on the ground at his site. He said that the landing site would remain lighted and that they would stop their tactical exercise, which we had no idea they were conducting.

After carefully returning to the site, I was met by American soldiers who took me to the patient. He did indeed have appendicitis. The American ground medic also informed me that they now had a second patient to deal with. This one was a German Army Special Forces captain wearing civilian clothes. He had a broken nose and a bad attitude.

Despite all the advantages that high-tech medical advances and state-of-the-art helicopters bring to saving lives, sometimes the more complex the capabilities are, the more possibilities there are for things to go wrong. An example of the old adage "what can go wrong, will go wrong" describes the following situation.

Besides a commitment to provide rescue and medical transport to the military throughout Europe, our unit was committed to providing the same for German civilians. The German EMS had its own rescue helicopters, both military and civilian. However, at this time, they were basically confined to flying in the daytime and in good weather. Our new helicopters could fly not only at night but also in bad weather; it did not take the German EMS folks long to realize this fact and to utilize it.

The night of this particular mission was a dark and rainy one. The pilots on duty consisted of a relatively new pilot who had recently been promoted from copilot and the copilot (my commander) who was a very experienced veteran pilot.

The new helicopter, with all its capabilities, was still a learning experience for both of these pilots. The old helicopter did not have the high-tech instrumentation of the new one. Because missions had to be completed in all kinds of weather, the pilots' workload increased from having to read the instruments—which were critical in keeping the helicopter flying when there were no visual outside references.

A request to immediately fly to a nearby town and meet an ambulance in a soccer field originated from the German emergency medical system. The cloud cover was so low that we had to sneak around and under the cloud deck on the way to the pickup site.

Upon landing and reaching the ambulance, I was informed by a German emergency medical technician (EMT) in his best English of the status of my patient. I assessed the patient's condition and attempted, in my best German, to assure him that I had correctly heard what the EMT had told me.

Much to my dismay, my interpretation of the patient's condition was correct. The patient had suffered a rupture of a major artery in his head. The EMT told me that the German doctors had given him a shot of Valium through his IV line in order to keep him unconscious. I was told that if not deeply unconscious, the patient would become combative because of the brain injury. One of the nightmare scenarios that can occur during a patient transfer is to have a violent, out-of-control individual loose in the helicopter.

A second bad scenario is to transport a patient with a head injury by helicopter, because even minor variations in altitude can have serious negative effects on a closed space (the skull) due to the related pressure changes encountered in flight.

The German EMT informed me that a German hospital that could treat severe brain injury was awaiting the patient. The hospital was approximately a forty-minute flight in distance. Patient requirements had to be considered when planning a patient transfer. Most of the times, this was accomplished prior to the mission. In dealing with our German friends, however, the system didn't always work as planned.

Because of the patient's injury, it was essential that he receive plenty of oxygen. I knew I had one hour's worth of oxygen on board the helicopter. The estimated flight time was forty minutes. That gave me a twenty-minute reserve of oxygen, which I did not perceive as a problem. I also had enough Valium to keep my patient unconscious for the flight. After loading the comatose patient, we departed into the rainy night sky.

The helicopter headed for the hospital after taking off. As it ascended into the night sky, it didn't take long to bump into the bottom of the clouds. By the time we were halfway to our destination, the clouds were so low we were forced to fly into them. Because we lost sight of the ground, we had to switch from visual flying to instrument flying. When an aircraft is forced by weather to make this kind of change, it must follow several defined procedures to ensure the safety of other aircraft already flying in the clouds. The aircraft must first climb to a predetermined altitude while simultaneously talking to an air-traffic controller to get further directions for orienting the aircraft.

At that point in the flight, two bad things had already happened regarding the care of my patient. First we were now forced to ascend in altitude to facilitate our handling by air traffic control. Remember that changes in altitude, especially increases, were bad for this patient's injury. Second, once you enter the air traffic control system, you become one of many aircraft using the system, and you often must wait to be given directions to proceed to a destination. As anyone who has flown commercially knows, you wait by flying in circles until it is your turn to land.

I was forced by circumstance to attend to my patient while our helicopter flew circles in the dark. Our ascent to a higher altitude had an immediate negative effect on my patient, requiring me to administer more Valium to maintain his relaxed/unconscious state.

Carefully I watched my patient's vital oxygen supply slowly diminish. I used the Valium the Germans supplied me as best I could to maintain the patient in an unconscious state. However, as it became more and more obvious that I would be caring for this patient longer than forty minutes and at a higher altitude than originally planned, I had to adjust by giving the patient less and less Valium each time he stirred.

Because of the weather, it was now impossible to take our patient to the original destination hospital. We had to return to the area near the site of the pickup to land at the airport under air traffic control. By now we were almost half an hour into the flight, and my oxygen and Valium supplies were steadily dwindling.

The pilot had earlier asked the ground controllers to find us a different hospital to take our patient to, but the ground controllers notified us that they were having trouble finding a local hospital that could accept a patient with his particular injuries.

Additionally, the German EMS would not send an ambulance to meet us at the airport until a hospital accepted the patient. Because of this, our helicopter was not given priority to land. The clock was running out on my oxygen and Valium reserves as we orbited in the darkness above the city.

My commander finally decided that our predicament was unacceptable, and he asked permission to descend below cloud level. After being granted this request and finding our bearings, we immediately headed for the large American military hospital located downtown. The pilot made several unsuccessful attempts to contact the military hospital to inform it of our intentions.

Just as we touched down on the hospital helipad, the last of my oxygen and Valium ran out. I left the patient with my crew chief while I ran into the hospital emergency room to get more supplies. The pilots and crew chief waited in the running helicopter for further instructions on where to bring the patient.

After I explained my predicament to the emergency department staff, they hurried to assist me with the supplies I had requested. As they were scurrying around for oxygen, the physician's assistant on duty in the emergency department wandered in and demanded to know what was going on.

As tactfully as I could, I proceeded to impress upon him my situation and the gravity of my patient's condition. Without batting an eye, the physician's assistant responded, as if from rote, that his facility did not care for German civilians.

As dumbstruck as I was by this blatant stupidity, I kept my cool, partly because our conversation was occurring in front of a waiting room full of already anxious people. I repeated my request for some replacement oxygen and Valium, and the physician's assistant, displaying how put out he was at this intrusion to his domain, reluctantly agreed to supply us with the oxygen. As far as the Valium was concerned, though, that was out of the question.

Just then, my crew chief came running through the emergency department doors. He was very anxious—our normally stoic commander was getting anxious—and, worse yet, the oxygen tank was empty and the patient was stirring. I had no trouble making a final decision concerning the deteriorating patient. I turned to my crew chief and several of the helpful staff and told them to follow me.

The physician's assistant asked me what I planned to do. I told him in front of the attentive waiting room audience that the circumstances he had placed me in gave me no choice but to turn over the care of my patient to a more qualified medical authority. I stated my medical opinion that for the immediate good of the patient, we needed to leave him at the hospital.

Despite the stutterings and protestations of the physician's assistant that he could not accept a German patient, I proceeded to inform my impatiently awaiting commander of the situation and of my decision. Unfortunately, before my commander (a Colonel) could impress upon the reluctant physician's assistant (a lieutenant) the forcefulness of my argument, a German ambulance showed up and assumed responsibility of our patient. I never learned the outcome of the patient involved. Sometimes you just never know if your skills and the benefits of technology can work to overcome all the obstacles that fate throws at you.

CHAPTER 6

The Deployment

A tiny island in the Mediterranean for
pitstop on the way to Desert Storm.

A stop in Egypt on the way to Saudia Arabia.

After Fort Drum, I was stationed back in Germany again for a staff job at the European Medevac Battalion. The medevac battalion consisted of three companies, each with twelve Blackhawk helicopters. I had been there approximately six months when the Iraqi invasion of Kuwait occurred. One of the battalion's medevac companies was selected to go to Saudi Arabia immediately after the invasion.

The usual method of long-distance military deployment of equipment and personnel was by US Air Force cargo transport. However, this method was not available to us due to the standing commitment to move combat personnel first to ensure a defense against a possible invasion of Saudi Arabia by the Iraqi forces already in Kuwait.

Our tasking, therefore, was to self-deploy. This deployment involved transporting to Kuwait, as rapidly as possible, twelve UH-60 Blackhawk medevac helicopters with crews of four each; all the support equipment required to accomplish the long self-deployment; and enough supplies to sustain us for as long as two weeks once we arrived.

This would be a world record helicopter flight, with the highest powers in Washington following our progress. The trip would be made by two separate groups of six helicopters each. Two of the six helicopters in each deployment would be equipped with extra fuel tanks and rescue hoists in case an aircraft went down over the vast stretches of water we would fly over.

It must be stated here that within days of our deployment notification, the helicopters chosen to deploy were swarmed over by our own and contracted technicians. The latest in navigation and radio electronics were fitted and checked out.

While these upgrades were occurring, the few members of our unit who had any desert and/or night-vision training were enlisted to train the other deploying crew members in these two essential arts. This pre-deployment activity kept me busy almost around the clock.

Because we were deploying to the desert, it was decided that in addition to ail the required military equipment that had literally been stuffed into the helicopters, cases of bottled water would be squeezed in as well. In my opinion, the rear compartment of each helicopter already was packed with too much equipment. The only way to fit in the additional and essential water was to pack it around the crew chief and medic in the back of the helicopter.

In Germany, at that time, the only bottled water available was in glass bottles. Now due to our plentiful water supply, we were resigned to death by flying glass in a simple hard landing. This thought caused much concern for the medics and crew chiefs who had to sit in the rear compartment of the helicopters.

We left on the twenty-first of September from Darmstadt, Germany. Our six Blackhawk helicopters were the second flight of a two six-helicopter deployment. Despite all the updated equipment installed on these helicopters, they did not have the capability to refuel in flight.

The helicopters had enough fuel to fly about two-and-one-half hours on a full tank. Therefore, we were required to be on the ground to refuel every two-and-one-half hours all the way to Saudi Arabia. The political and logistical efforts applied to allow us to traverse half the world by helicopter must be applauded. As I previously stated, the resources brought to bear for the accomplishment of our mission were amazing if not occasionally overkill.

The route of flight required us to fly into and out of numerous countries. We had to receive permission from a country to land; refuel; and, at some locations, rest overnight. On occasion, the host nations' airports were taken by surprise when our foreign group of helicopters descended upon them. However, each and every one of the host nations was completely hospitable once they discovered our intentions.

The initial route of flight took us over the German, Austrian, and Italian Alps. Germany and Italy had active US military bases in their countries and allowed us to land, while Austria did not. Our first two days were spent flying to the tip of Italy. Refueling the aircraft and ourselves always occurred in a rush as we hopped from one military base to another.

Up to this point, the journey had gone by the numbers. On the very last leg of our trip to the tip of Italy, however, one of the helicopters developed a serious vibration in flight. The pilots noticed that the vibration diminished if they flew the aircraft slower than normal. As luck would have it, the rescue unit's maintenance officer was flying the malfunctioning aircraft. He noticed that one of the four main rotor blades was not tracking like the other three and was spinning lower. This caused the vibration in flight.

The helicopter limped into our last stop in Italy just before dark. Before the helicopter blades had even stopped turning, the problem was identified. A portion of the outer skin of the suspect main rotor blade had come apart from the core material on the inside of the blade. This caused a large bubble or blister to form which, in turn, upset the airflow of the affected rotor blade and caused the vibration.

It was obvious that we could not continue across the Mediterranean Sea with this helicopter until we got a replacement main rotor blade. Considering the pre-deployment availability of resources, we anticipated a positive response to our maintenance request and assumed the military would fly-in a replacement blade. Had we considered the reason for our ordered self-deployment, the reply to our response could have been anticipated.

The system already was taxed to the point where twelve rescue helicopters had to self-deploy halfway around the world. The response to our request for a part was to fix it; no replacement blade would be forthcoming. Cypress was the closest location that could deliver us a new rotor blade. That city, however, was at the other end of our Mediterranean crossing.

Faced with this dilemma, the entire group switched to "MacGyver mode" without blinking an eye. Left to the ingeniousness of our own devices, the blade was removed from the helicopter for repair within a matter of minutes. An ingenious solution was contrived and implemented even before darkness fell.

We decided to drill small holes in the bubbled outer skin. This was accomplished using the punch of a Swiss army knife. Next, a super epoxy was injected into the cavity between the skin and the core of the blade using a medical syringe. Finally, cases of military food rations were piled upon the repaired area and strapped down as weight to force the skin to adhere back to the core. All there remained to do that night was to eat some hot food and get a few hours of sleep.

The morning was a bright, clear, southern Mediterranean one. Before the sun was full in the sky, our truly remarkable maintenance officer and his crew had remounted the "fixed" main rotor blade and satisfactorily test-flown the helicopter. The helicopter was declared repaired with the exception of a little wobble in flight, and the decision was made to continue on without delay.

At this point, I must admit that I was glad the "fixed" helicopter was not mine. The next series of stops were located between vast stretches of ocean, a reminder of why two of our six helicopters had extra fuel tanks and rescue hoists; if a helicopter went down over water, the outfitted helicopters could perform a rescue and still make the next refueling stop.

One particular stretch of ocean would take approximately two hours and fifteen minutes to cross. This gave the helicopters without external fuel tanks only fifteen minutes of flight time to spare before landing at our remote island destination or splashing into the sea.

Actually, the latter was preferred by the guys in the back as opposed to crashing on land. A softer crash might spare us from being cut to ribbons by all the glass bottles of water packed around us.

One remote refueling location in the vast Mediterranean was a tiny island. This rock sticking out of the ocean was just long enough to hold a runway and a small support facility. Both runway overruns stopped at precipices over the ocean. The airstrip appeared to be cut out of the flat side of an old volcano or seamount.

Awaiting us on cue were three army CH-47 cargo helicopters. Each had a large cargo bay full of rubber tanks filled with helicopter fuel for our aircraft. We landed in line along the length of the runway and refueled our helicopters three at a time.

This was accomplished without shutting down any of the helicopters. It was accomplished so swiftly that our crew members had just enough time to shake a few hands in thanks and snap a few pictures, and then we were off. We were now heading east toward Cypress, our next overnight stop and the location of our replacement rotor blade.

All the helicopters circled in to land at the Cypress International Airport just after dark. Immediately upon parking and shutting down the helicopters, the damaged blade was replaced. The local authorities were most gracious; however, they insisted that we change from our flight suits into civilian clothing before we left the airport tarmac. Although worn-out, we graciously consented to our hosts' request and stripped out of our flight suits right there under the floodlights on the airport tarmac. We put on extremely wrinkled civilian attire in order to blend in, boarded our bus, and were driven to a hillside villa for an evening's rest.

Our next stop upon leaving the Mediterranean behind us was Egypt. Due to diplomatic requirements, a Blackhawk helicopter from the US Embassy in Cairo escorted us to our first stop in Egypt. Because the embassy helicopter had to land first, the crew chief on board that helicopter decided to guide the other six helicopters into their respective parking spots. Excited by his involvement in such an historic mission, the embassy crew chief was not taking care to maintain the appropriate distance between the helicopters he was parking.

As my helicopter taxied alongside an already parked helicopter that was in the process of shutting down, I could see that we were too close. The rotor disk on our helicopter was not outside the other helicopter's rotor disk but was turning above it. Because the other helicopter's rotor blades were slowing down, they had started to "droop" or to go from straight-out to bent when not turning. As I started to alert the pilot of the potential catastrophe about to unfold, he also became aware of the embassy crew chief's error.

Because our helicopter was still running at flight speed, the rotor blades were still sticking straight out. The pilot very smoothly and cautiously lifted the helicopter up and backward until the rotor disks were separated. His correct assessment of the situation and action in the blink of an eye saved the entire mission, as all seven helicopters were parked right next to each other. The flying metal and explosions that would have occurred had the two helicopters' rotor blades enmeshed would have destroyed all the helicopters and killed many crewmen, including myself.

In my own defense, I will now say that it had already been a long-and-tiring deployment. My actions following this close call were therefore justified if just a little bit rash. I informed the pilots that I was exiting the helicopter and received their approval.

After disconnecting myself from my communication cord and carefully walking out from under the slowing rotor blades, I commenced to chase that *stupid* son-of-a-bitch crew chief into the desert with the intent of killing him as soon as I caught him.

Seeing my obvious intent, the pilot sent my crew chief to restrain me. After several other individuals joined in, they managed to pry me off my intended victim. Later that evening at dinner, I approached the commander of my intended victim and offered my apologies for the afternoon's excitement. He accepted my apology, then smiled and whispered that the embassy crew chief was lucky that someone had stopped me.

Our next stop after a night's rest in western Egypt was a landing just west of Cairo. The vastness of the Egyptian desert is far greater than that of the American desert. After hours of flying above the desert in all of its variations, from dune to escarpment, it was easy to believe no one could survive there. The conditions were so harsh that the crew members in the back of the helicopter were forced by the oppressive heat to leave their side windows open, figuring that hot blowing air was better than hot still air. To the crew members, this felt like a hair dryer blowing in their face all day long.

Some crew members experienced nosebleeds due to the 150-mile-an-hour crosswind of hot, dry, blowing desert air. We overcame this dilemma by using our precious bottled water to constantly soak medical slings that we wore on our faces as kerchiefs. This moistened the hot air and stopped the nosebleeds. We employed this technique the entire time we flew across the Arabian Desert.

I should stop here and describe what the military required us to wear at a minimum during flight. From head to toe, the military had equipped us for safety: a lined flight helmet, a long-sleeved Nomex flight suit, an over-vest full of survival equipment, and high leather boots—just the ensemble for long, hot days in the desert.

The pilots saw it first—the famous green strip of life that runs along the Nile. As we flew over the desert at 150 miles an hour at a few hundred feet off the ground, we had watched the vast desert slide by. Now there was green as far as the eye could see stretching out in a thin line into the distance. We flashed over small fields and villages. The grass was coarse and thick, and the palms grew wild and in rows. Then we were over the suburbs of what could have been any foreign city, and there were highways and roads.

I stuck my head out the side window, bearing the brunt of the wind to look ahead as the pilots exclaimed. There was Cairo, a shining city in the wavering heat of the midday desert. Behind it in the haze, I could see the Great Pyramids. As we flew by Cairo en route to our final stop in Egypt, we circled the Great Pyramids. No one, as far as I knew, asked if we could or if we should; we all just silently did it.

Our final destination in Egypt was a short refueling stop at an Egyptian airfield on the banks of the Red Sea. After my years in the desert, I thought I had seen some remote, god-awful places. This stretch of ancient desert, though, was the new prizewinner.

Immediately after shutting the helicopters down and stepping out to stretch our legs, our Egyptian military hosts appeared with very old wooden soda cases. The cases were filled with long-neck soda bottles that were so old the areas of the bottles that protruded were ground opaque from repeated use. With a gracious smile and a little reluctance, we accepted and drank the offered soft drinks.

Awaiting certain intestinal difficulties after consuming our hosts' parting gift, it was off across the Red Sea. The water crossing was a well-deserved blessing from the constant in-flight convection oven that was the desert. The sea was remarkably clear, and the air over the sea was cool. The anxiety of flying over water without land in sight, which had been the case during the Mediterranean crossing, was replaced by a wish to continue this cool, beautiful excursion as long as possible.

Too soon, though, the western coast of Saudi Arabia appeared on the horizon. The first thing we noticed after crossing the endless stretch of desert beach was that the desert was different on this side of the Red Sea. The interior western coast of Saudi Arabia can be described as fairly mountainous. The colors of the desert are more varied and irregular than on the western side of the Red Sea. The hills and mountains are very rugged and dark in color. Thankfully this variation in the terrain below had a cooling effect on the air we were flying through.

Our first stop in Saudi Arabia was just before dark at a Saudi military/civilian airport. Dinner was served late at a Saudi military dining facility. The delightful hot meal of chicken and salad would come back to haunt us all.

As we would soon find out, this combination would be served every night for months to come. In the morning, we lined up to depart and head inland into the rising sun. Our departure was momentarily delayed due to an inbound Saudi commercial jet declaring an emergency landing because one engine was out. The commercial airplane landed safely; however, it left me with an ominous feeling as we flew into the Saudi desert.

Another essential piece of flight gear that was improvised came into being at this time. When landing a helicopter in sand, it is essential to keep moving forward until the wheels touch down. To ensure that the area below was clear of obstacles, the crew members in the back had to open their windows, stick their heads out, and look forward and down to assist the pilots in landing.

Whenever they did this, however, their eyes and unexposed faces were sandblasted by the Arabian Desert sand—which is larger and coarser than that of either the American or Egyptian deserts. The solution came out of a crew chief's toolbox. We began wearing the plastic grinder's goggles that were issued in each toolbox. These worked the best because you could still lower the helmet visor, or wear sunglasses underneath them. Even the night vision goggles fit over them. Our ensemble was now complete, and the sight of us scared the hell out of more than one Saudi airman as we traversed the desert.

The next and last overnight stay before reaching our final destination was the Saudi capital of Riyadh. Dinner was again chicken and salad. Following dinner, there was a short congratulatory presentation along with a briefing by the US military command at Riyadh. The next morning, bright and early, we were on our way for a fifth day into the rising sun. After a short refueling stop, we landed at our final destination.

CHAPTER 7

The Gulf War

Original patch Desert
shield/Storm.

What you do before the tents show up? cargo chute. Improvisation is mandatory when your first in Country.

My experience in Saudi Arabia lasted, just short of a year, from August 1990 to July 1991. Dhahran, Saudi Arabia, is a large city located on the Persian Gulf. It became our center of operations and was the one place I tried to stay away from.

After taxing off the runway, we were directed to our parking spots on the tarmac, right next to the remnants of the Kuwait Air Force that had escaped to this airfield during the invasion of Kuwait. Our billeting at this permanent location was a hanger used to paint airplanes. After five days of flying halfway across the world, we opened our cots and finally got some rest. This new home became very crowded in the first few days as additional support personnel started to arrive by military airlift.

The first tasking to come down for our unit was for two helicopters and their crews, with radio communications and all necessary equipment, to self-deploy to a remote spot along a major road supply route ninety flying miles from Dhahran. There we set up to respond to any rescue requests that occurred along this route as troops and equipment poured in from the coast to inland positions.

The only US military medical facility on the east coast of Saudi Arabia was an Air Force evacuation center set up on the tarmac at the airport in Dhahran. This meant that any patients who were rescued anywhere in the country had to be brought back to Dhahran. This trip at top speed took about an hour. The medical facility consisted of a large treatment tent and several smaller support tents. The facility's objective was to accept patients from our helicopters and hold them until an Air Force plane arrived to fly the patients to a military hospital located in Europe.

Looking for any excuse to get out of the paint hanger, I immediately volunteered for this first assignment. The next morning, we prepared to deploy forward into the desert. My job on the morning of our departure was to go over to the Air Force medical facility to coordinate our activities. The pilots were busy planning the flight and studying the area of our deployment, while the rest of the crew were preparing the necessary equipment.

Due to numerous delays, most of them involving our superiors, we did not actually depart until late afternoon. The flight to our new home was uneventful as we flew into the setting sun. As we approached our chosen landing site, however, the sun had already dipped below the horizon.

In the desert, this meant that in a few moments, conditions went from lightness and long shadows to darkness. The change in light caused the second helicopter to have difficulty landing. It took three nervous approaches to the landing site to accomplish a landing. This capped our frustration at being delayed back at the airport in Dhahran.

Now that both of our helicopters were safely on the ground, it was time to set up camp in the dark. As I had been at the Air Force medical facility during the equipment loading, I did not know we were deploying forward without tents. Tents apparently were in short supply back in the growing military city that was Dhahran. We decided to deploy without tents for the time being and were assured that on our next visit, a tent would be available. Forty million dollars in helicopters and equipment, and we couldn't get a tent.

That first night, we opened our cots under the helicopters and sat around a small propane fire heating some coffee, surrounded by the desert night's impenetrable darkness. As we sat there relaxing for the first time in weeks, we heard someone approaching on foot in the desert blackness. Now I had flown into this remote location before dark. I knew there was no one out there in the middle of nowhere. We all had side arms with us; however, like every good soldier with no war experience, the bullets were in the helicopter.

Anyway, by the time we heard the approaching footsteps, it was too late to do anything but stand up. Slowly our guest appeared to us. First the sandals on his feet came into view. Then as he came closer, we saw the white robe of a Bedouin—a desert nomad. Anxiety turned to relief at the site of our new neighbor. He strolled right up with a smile and with his hand raised in a friendly gesture. You would have thought he saw Americans and helicopters every day.

He squatted down at our pathetic little fire and, without a word, bummed a cigarette, which he very much enjoyed. We shared a cup of coffee with our nocturnal visitor, but he did not seem to think too much of that. With a word of thanks in Arabic and a slight bow, he disappeared back into the desert blackness as easily as he had arrived. This first encounter with a local inhabitant affected us all.

The next morning, our helicopter flew to our base in Dhahran to get more equipment, supplies, and maybe a tent. The good news was that the folks back at the base had managed to fill two big coolers with ice for us to bring back to the desert. The bad news was that they still could not supply us with a tent.

Desperation would once again lead to inspiration as I looked for a supplement to our missing tent. A tent in the desert is even more necessary than one elsewhere. Remember, it's not rain that makes a tent necessary in the desert but protection from the intense sun.

As a former survival instructor for the Air Force, I was familiar with making shelters and knew that a parachute made a great survival shelter in the desert. However, helicopters didn't carry parachutes. Also, a parachute would make a great shelter for one or two people, but we needed shelter for eight crew members and a radio operator. The answer was a big parachute.

At the air base back in Dhahran, the Air Force was moving men and equipment at an incredible rate. As a result, all kinds of equipment were lying around. I found just what I was looking for: a huge green military cargo parachute used for parachuting things like tanks. After quickly explaining my dilemma to an astonished Air Force sergeant, who couldn't take his eyes off my flight attire, he not only agreed to assist me but also drove me back to my unit.

All I needed now were some tent poles. In true form, finding tent poles was not a problem. On the contrary, it appeared that the army had more tent poles than it could ever use. It just didn't have enough tents. I still had difficulty getting permission to take the tent poles that I needed.

Our unit's supply sergeant, who had just arrived by military transport, could not justify relinquishing the requested poles without an accompanying tent—of which there were none available. Eventually I acquired the needed tent poles. The only remaining obstacle was to convince my fellow crew members that this was a good idea as opposed to waiting for the requested tent to be issued.

After literally drawing the proposed shelter design and reminding everyone of our present track record of tent procurement, I convinced the crew that this was our best hope for a tent in the near future.

The shelter was constructed at our new forward base the next morning. It was designed with the parachute folded in half. A large ten-foot tent pole was placed in the center of the parachute, which was positioned to afford the most protection from the sun during the hottest part of the day. It had the form of a three-quarter Indian teepee. The opening of the shelter faced west, and the curve of the parachute arched from north to south.

The shelter was constructed so that the inner and outer halves of the folded parachute were separated to create dead air space in between. This dead air space caused an inner cooling of the shelter. Smaller tent poles were used to elevate the ends of the parachute to provide us with airflow and more living space.

Our new home was an instant hit with the crews, and it made me very proud. The status of our forward quarters grew to the point where we were receiving visitors, high ranking and otherwise, who wanted to see our setup for themselves.

Our difficulties in acquiring shelter would lead us to all kinds of mischief. For want of a more permanent shelter as the weather turned colder, we utilized the distraction of a severe desert sand storm to carry off a large Bedouin tent that was sitting in an army supply center.

We received our first medevac request a day or two following deployment. An army van had driven off the highway and flipped over several times before coming to rest on its right side. Of the two people in the vehicle, one was dead at the scene and the other had critical internal injuries. The helicopter landed about twenty yards from the accident scene. The temperature was 128 degrees at that time of day.

Because of the patient's injuries, I had to repeatedly send my crew chief back to the helicopter for more medical equipment. By the third trip, he said, "Look, if I have to make another trip, you're going to have another patient here!" He looked pale and sweaty, a look I had seen many times during my years in the American desert. I decided to rest my crew chief and utilize the people at the crash scene to help move the patient back to the helicopter.

As we were preparing to depart the scene with our critically injured patient, some soldiers who had gathered at the scene delayed me momentarily. They wanted me to load the dead-accident victim on the helicopter. I informed them that I was desperately trying to keep a man alive for the sixty-minute flight to Dhahran and could not waste the time it would take to load a dead man. I was successful in both convincing the soldiers of my logic and in getting my patient back to Dhahran alive.

That evening, I was ordered to report to a colonel to officially explain why I had left the body of an officer out in the desert. Only after the colonel was satisfied with my answer did he congratulate me for saving the life of the enlisted man.

As preparations for the coming war expanded, so did our rescue responsibilities. Another mission assignment that was unique to us, involved the transfer of patients and supplies to the pair of newly arrived hospital ships. These ships were stationed out in the Persian Gulf. One of our most demanding mission was to rescue a patient from the middle of the desert in the middle of the night, fly over hundreds of miles of ocean, and then land on a brightly lit floating hospital.

I have been discussing throughout this book the difficulties of flying at night and the use of night-vision goggles. The desert environment of southwest Asia turned out to be the most challenging I had ever experienced with respect to night flying.

The combination of haze and dust in the air restricted visibility at the best of times. Wind- and sandstorms kicked up day or night without much warning. The particles in the air reduced what little depth perception there was wearing the goggles to practically zero. We were required to fly as low as possible and always below five hundred feet above the ground.

Lastly, the following elements of all medevac missions increased the challenge: speed was of the essence, and we were always flying alone. There could be no doubt that the medevac crews put themselves at risk more often than anyone else during the Gulf War, with the possible exception of the Air Force combat pilots who occasionally called on us for a ride home after a bad day at the office.

Nighttime rescues during the Gulf War ranged from the routinely harrowing to the fatal. Regardless of which phase of the conflict we were involved with, the catastrophic potential was always right over our shoulders. To illustrate this, I will describe a night-mission profile that occurred regularly. A rescue request would come in shortly before midnight. On some occasions, we would be anticipating the call and would just relax and wait, trying not to think about it. Once the request was received, things happened very quickly. The crew members would rush to the helicopter to prepare it for takeoff. The pilots would receive final tactical intelligence and plan the routes.

When the pilots arrived at the helicopter, they would strap right in and prepare for takeoff. Many times the flight medic and crew chief didn't know the details of the mission until the helicopter was already on its way. After takeoff, the pilots would brief us on the mission while we made final adjustments to our night-vision goggles and other equipment.

The initial route from our current base was always predetermined for security purposes. Therefore, this would be the most composed and routine part of the flight. Once the helicopter was out of the usual flight route, it would descend, speed up, and start to fly close to the ground to avoid detection and to stay below the allied fighter aircraft above.

The job of the crew members in the back of the helicopter during this flight mode would be to continuously scan the horizon on each side of the helicopter for any obstacle or other bad thing that might interfere with the helicopter's flight; I have already described the limitations of vision while using the night-vision devices.

The view outside the side windows where the crew members would sit was restricted to up, down, and forward. A large external fuel tank positioned directly outside the side window would prevent us from looking straight out at the horizon. We would desperately peer out at the hazy green world flashing by us, trying to spot some as yet invisible power line or high sand dune, or worse.

When we spotted something, we would try to track it to determine its location to the helicopter. Since depth perception was very limited, the only way we could verify an object's size and distance was to watch it as the helicopter moved in relation to it. This process would continue until we reached the rescue site. I have already described the intensity of landing in the desert at night. Suffice it to say that during my time flying around the Gulf at night, my helicopter ran across a road, over a refueling point, and into an unseen sand dune during night landings.

Finally jolting to a stop, the halo of glowing sand created by the spinning rotor blades would be the first thing we saw. The goal at this stage of the rescue would be to spend as little time on the ground as possible. A swarm of green faces would rush at us—a vibrant series of snapshots displaying varying degrees of panic, trauma, and blood. We would organize enough semi-panicked people to help load the patients and then fly out even faster than when we came in.

Next I would care for the patients while trying to clear my side of the helicopter from dangers. The disadvantage of night-vision goggles was that you could not see anything that was closer than eighteen inches. Over and over again I would look under my goggles and use a red light to treat the patients and then look through my goggles to clear the helicopter in flight. In the meantime, the helicopter would be pitching and rolling as the pilots made the best speed for our destination.

One night, our destination was a hospital ship floating 150 miles off the coast of Saudi Arabia. After flying right above the ground for at least twenty minutes, the flight smoothed out once we were over the Persian Gulf. As we looked through our night-vision goggles, all we could see was an occasional whitish-green wavy line. The helicopter pilots relied on a series of radio signals to find the hospital ship in the middle of the Persian Gulf in the middle of the night.

The hospital ship was required by Geneva Convention Law to be illuminated at night, and the ship's glow could be seen from well over the horizon. After hours of intense flying using night-vision devices, we approached the small helipad of the hospital ship without the goggles. The transition back to a bright white world with peripheral vision was always startling.

The navy crew secured the helicopter to the deck with "chalks and chains" immediately after it touched down. Then under bright white lights, the navy litter teams—who were dressed in white shirts for identification on deck—unloaded the patients from the helicopter. I finally got a good look at their faces. While the helicopter was being refueled on deck, I accompanied my patients to the receiving ward and briefed the staff on their status.

On that night, while my patients were being unloaded, I stepped forward of the helicopter to get out of the way. As I watched the unloading, I turned my head to look over the side of the ship. I was so disoriented by the previous flight that the effect of vertigo on my already unsteady equilibrium made me fall right over on my side. This did not go unnoticed by the people on deck, who thought it was the funniest thing they had ever seen. After slowly regaining my feet, I carefully walked to the door of the ship, smiling sheepishly.

The helicopter was refueled and was ready to depart by the time I finished my briefing. Replacement supplies and litters were placed onboard the helicopter, and we headed back toward shore. Once the lights of the ship faded behind us, it was time to go back to the little green world of night vision.

Inbound back to our forward base, we were notified that we had to divert south to our headquarters for some minor reason or other. We arrived back in the white-lit nighttime world of Dhahran. Our business at headquarters took us just long enough to allow an early breakfast at the military dining facility.

As we staggered in, the looks we got reminded me of the Joe and Willie comics of the second world war. I bore those looks with a combination of resentment for the rear-area guys and pride at being a more direct part of the war than they could even imagine. We savored our breakfast as best we could in the time we had to eat it. Then it was back to the helicopter for a short ninety-mile daytime flight to our forward base to await the next call.

Not all the missions were of this length and intensity. Some were longer and easier, and some were shorter and more frightening. Whether long or short, too many of the missions ended with the crew members wide awake and trying to catch their breath hours after a safe return to base.

CHAPTER 8

Kuwait

Kuwait helicopter rescue and Explosiv Ordnance Disposal

Kuwait record of CMS rescues سي أم أس

28 APR 93

To: Whom it may concern.

Subject: Employment History Operation "Desert Sweep"

I certify that between the dates of 3 May 92 and 17 May 93, Mr. Michael J. Disario was employed as a Flight-Paramedic under my direction and that the following medical training academic and clinical, and patient care on-scene and transport was accomplished.

Medical Training:
American Heart Assoc. BLS-C (ref.)
American Heart Assoc. ACLS (ref.)
60 hours of continuing medical education covering the following topics:
Acute trauma care.
Acute burn care.
Advanced airway management.
Trauma management pharmacology.
Intravenous fluid applications and management.
Triage management.
Cardiac emergency management.
Aeromedical physiology.
Aeromedical operations.

Patient Care: The following lists the individual trauma cases treated and transported by date and nature of injury.
07 Jun 92 - Traumatic amputation, blast and fragmentation.
15 Jun 92 - Multiple fragmentation, internal, blast.
15 Jun 92 - Multiple fragmentation, internal, blast.
22 Jun 92 - Miocardial infarction.
22 Jun 92 - Open fracture, crushing.
09 Sep 92 - Fragmentation, blast.
12 Sep 92 - Multiple fragmentation, internal, blast.
22 Oct 92 - Multiple fragmentation, internal, blast.
11 Oct 92 - Fragmentation, blast.
01 Nov 92 - Fractured femur, internal injuries.
16 Jan 93 - Traumatic amputation, blast.
26 Jan 93 - Traumatic amputation, fragmentation, blast.
26 Mar 93 - Multiple amputation, total body trauma, blast.
26 Mar 93 - Multiple fragmentation, internal, blast.
15 Apr 93 - Traumatic amputation, blast.

Dr. Wajih M. Eida,
Physician CMS-I

DR WAJIAH EIDA
CMS I
AL MANOF 3722468

I returned to Germany following the Gulf War. Soon afterward, an old friend of mine contacted me about a special job in Kuwait. He stated that a civilian company in Florida was looking for a flight paramedic to support an international construction project to rid post-war Kuwait of Iraqi explosives, ammunitions, and equipment left over after the conflict.

The army decided after the war that it had too many soldiers, and it offered incentive bonuses to people who would volunteer to leave the service. This was all the incentive I needed, as the job offer in Kuwait involved a large sum of money as well. I suppose this decision clearly classifies me as more of a mercenary than a loyal soldier. So be it.

Because of this new opportunity, my stay at home in Germany only lasted six months. My old partner during the war, who also had been hired for the project, met me at the airport in Kuwait City. This time, the living conditions in the Persian Gulf were quite agreeable.

We were housed in a beachside condo tower with all the amenities of maid service, dining facility, laundry, etc. The dwellings were a pair of high-rise towers with an underground garage, patio, and pool. Each apartment was fully equipped and furnished. Each had three bedrooms, a living room with balcony overlooking the ocean, two baths, and a complete kitchen. Every morning, breakfast was served American style in the main dining area. Food to make a lunch was supplied after breakfast, and a full dinner was served every night.

I mention the accommodations first because they were the main advantage of being in this war-torn country. The personnel hired for this unique project would certainly earn the accommodations they were provided, as well as the salaries they were paid.

We worked six days a week. The day started before sunup to get a jump on the searing heat of the day. The crews in the field could not start their dangerous work until the rescue assets were in place. This meant that the helicopter crew had to be at the airport each and every workday. The workday lasted until the light, the heat, or a desert storm stopped work for that day. Not until the last person had left the work area for the day could the rescue folks go home.

In this job, the occasional occupational hazard was being blown to bits. Or if you got off lucky, losing a limb. I discovered that I was one of almost four hundred mostly American, ex-military, and new employees for a company that had won the contract to *completely* demilitarize the post-war country of Kuwait. The contract specified that every remaining piece of military hardware and materials left on Kuwait's soil after the conflict had to be removed. This formidable task included removing not only Iraqi munitions and equipment but coalition remnants as well.

I am convinced that every single foot of Kuwait had a small coalition bomb on it at one time or another. For the Iraqi's part, I must commend them on their outstanding ability to move large numbers of munitions in a short period of time. In six months' time, the amount of munitions that had been moved south to Kuwait was absolutely astonishing. The contract also stipulated that the desert had to be returned to its pre-war state. This meant that all tanks and other military vehicles had to be removed and all Iraqi bunkers and fortifications had to be dismantled. The real battle in post-war Kuwait, though, was removing the land mines. Minefields stretched as far as the eye could see.

My new employer had undertaken this unprecedented task by hiring every explosive ordinance disposal (EOD) person it could find. Age, former military service, or geographic location on the planet made no difference. They were found, were enticed by a great sum of money, and were whisked off to Kuwait just like me. I found myself

93

in this group of extremely *unique* individuals not for my knowledge of explosives but for my medical knowledge of what explosives could do to the human body.

A grand total of eight medical personnel had been hired as lifesavers for a crew of almost four hundred people. There was only one company doctor. His chief responsibility was to treat the company employees for minor injuries and illnesses.

The remainder of the medical team consisted of a senior medical advisor who served as the liaison between the field medics and the Kuwaiti hospitals and seven strategically stationed paramedics on the ground. Each drove a desert vehicle equipped with a radio, a global-positioning system, and a complete paramedic kit.

The idea was for the paramedics to respond to an injury and to utilize their medical equipment to stabilize and prepare the patient for air evacuation. The helicopter would then arrive and unload the onboard paramedic kit, load the "packaged" patient, and continue treatment in flight while flying the patient to an awaiting Kuwaiti hospital.

This medical service was available to all company employees, American or otherwise (the contract employed workers from many nations). The contract also included medical coverage for an English EOD project adjacent to ours.

The medevac crew waited for radio calls at an office at the Kuwait International Airport. The daily assignment required that the medevac crew be within three minutes of takeoff at all times. The crew consisted of a pilot and a crew chief in the front two seats and the flight medic in the back for a total of three crew members.

In all my years in the helicopter business, I had never met or flown with a more experienced pilot than when I flew in Kuwait. His experience could only be described as legendary. The crew chief was an old Gulf Coast oilrig helicopter repairman. His experience in fixing helicopters in remote locations was vast. However, he was a rookie in the rescue-end of the business.

The benefactors of our participation in this undertaking were the folks whose daily job it was to find and destroy all the munitions that had not already done their destructive work during the war. The chain-of-brotherhood of these individuals was as unique as their profession. It allowed a few members of this group to mobilize men from their mid-twenties to their mid-sixties in age. The combat experience encompassed every United States conflict since World War II. The positions of responsibility held by these individuals reached the highest levels of our government, including presidential protection.

However, these same shining products of our best military training institutes were, soon after arriving, scolded by our project manager for organizing a competition of daring involving multiple balconies and a swimming pool. The command staff of this construction project consisted of retired military officers with military engineering and logistical backgrounds. These gentlemen would certainly have their collective hands full supervising and living in the same buildings with these special technicians.

The first day on the job consisted of orientation to the new system, including a crash course in military explosives of the world. The next morning after breakfast, I was introduced to the pilot and crew chief of the medevac helicopter which would take me out to the airport for my first day. The helicopter was a UH-1 Huey like the ones I had flown at Fort Irwin, except that this one was a later model with two engines.

The interior of the helicopter, especially the crew compartment, was the same as the earlier model. I discovered that my new office space was primitive in its amenities. I could not complain, however, as my daily cell for the next twelve months was, after all, air-conditioned. My colleagues were fond of reminding me that although they certainly appreciated my presence, I was in no position to grumble about my place of work.

Due to the day's heat in this part of the world, the workday started hours before dawn and ended before the unbearable heat of the day really got going. The pilot and crew chief started the morning helicopter preflight and run up. I completed an orientation and preflight of the helicopter and equipment while the run up was in progress. After being satisfied with the status of the helicopter, we went back to our office to get better acquainted.

As part of the operational procedure, we were required to report that the helicopter was ready before daily operations in the field could begin. Conversely, we could not leave the airport until the last workers were accounted for and had returned to the towers. Additionally, we were required to constantly monitor the radios in our office. These radios carried all the radio traffic between the various teams in the field. An instantaneous answer to a request for air evacuation, followed by a takeoff in less than three minutes, was a no-fail requirement.

On this first morning, we had just come back to the office. As we were settling in, the crackle of radio traffic was broken by a voice requesting immediate medical help. It was that tone of voice that is more forceful and anxious, and which actually sounds louder than the rest of the traffic. It was an Englishman's voice trying to contain the panic we could hear rising in his tone.

Everyone on the air heard it at the same time, instantly all the chatter stopped, and the radio stayed quiet except for communications between the helicopter and the ground during the mission. All fieldwork immediately stopped not just because of the radio usage priority but because the only rescue asset was now busy. It was not a good idea to mess with explosives when the medevac helicopter was otherwise engaged.

The voice came in with lots of static and was very faint, but the request was unmistakable; and the news was not good. As we rushed to the helicopter, we listened to the details of the request on a portable radio. As soon as the pilot turned on the helicopter radios, he acknowledged the request. We departed the airport directly from our parking spot on the tarmac.

We headed toward our destination, flying as fast as the helicopter would go. The information coming in from the request site could not have been any more shocking, even to me! A crew of five laborers under the supervision of an

English EOD technician had been loading explosives into a large dump truck. They had been working in an Iraqi ammunition supply point (ASP), a storage facility for all the explosives in the Iraqi military inventory. The types of explosives included land mines, mortar and artillery ammunition, hand grenades, and others. All these explosives had been sitting in the desert for almost three years. The desert's dry climate and wide temperature variations could cause many of these explosives to become unstable.

The supervisor had been sitting in the cab of the dump truck while a team of five laborers in the bed of the dump truck passed and stacked the various military explosives. One laborer was standing behind the dump truck and was handing up explosives that were scattered on the ground all over the ASP. Some piece of an unstable explosive device, or perhaps a random spark or an act of God, caused the entire load to detonate simultaneously.

The radio exposed the growing pandemonium at the scene as more people arrived. As we approached our destination, we could see that the ASP had a large explosive crater in the middle of it. A group of people scurried around this crater, which had several large pieces of blackened, twisted metal lying around it. The largest of these pieces was the remainder of the back axle of the dump truck.

As I stepped out after touching down, I noticed someone approaching me. He was being very careful where he was walking. I assumed this was because of the unexploded munitions lying around. The EOD technician was used to walking around explosives, however, and this was not what made him watch his step. He was being careful not to step on the many scattered pieces of human body lying everywhere.

The wind and dust raised by the helicopter had died down, and I could survey the scene. Scattered in front of me among the blackened earth and metal were many variously sized and shaped cleanly cut body pieces. There were no body parts, just neatly sliced pieces—some as large as a breadbox. I turned toward my crew to see if they could see what I saw. My pilot looked at me in shock, while my crew chief—who had no medevac experience—was holding on to the cockpit door with both hands.

I needed my crew chief to help me carry some medical gear. We had gone over the equipment and procedures that morning, and I yelled at him to grab the extra medical gear and follow me. He just stood there on the landing skid looking down at his feet, a white-knuckle grip on the helicopter door. He was shaking his head back and forth in a no-way gesture. He had seen enough medevac stuff for the day, and maybe for good.

The English medics at the scene led me toward two survivors. On the way to the patients, I observed another English medic running toward the scene. Before reaching us, he tripped over something and almost fell. The object was large, and I thought that it was part of the truck. I was wrong. It was one of the larger body pieces of the workers who had been in the back of the truck.

After surveying the scene, I could not believe that anyone had survived the explosion. Amazingly, though, the supervisor and the laborer on the ground had survived. An English medic led me to the supervisor first as he was the most critically injured of the two survivors. His injuries were not immediately visible by the medics at the scene.

He had been thrown onto his back yards from his sitting position inside the cab of the truck. His injuries turned out to be fatal. His entire torso had been peppered with metal fragments from the explosion. All the entry wounds were in the back and were not noticeable because of the position of the patient. Because—upon arrival—the patient still had a pulse, resuscitation efforts were carried out all the way to the hospital.

Miraculously, the other survivor who had been standing directly behind the truck received only minor lacerations and burns besides a set of ruptured eardrums.

How could a large steel dump truck be completely blown away, the men standing inside it blown to bits, and yet a man standing right behind the truck be left almost completely unscathed? With the help of the English medics at the scene, I loaded my two survivors on board. On the way back, I struggled to resuscitate one patient and calm the other. This first day at work would prepare me for the days ahead.

The last entry I will make in this medevac log is the one that haunts me the most; it involved a rescue from one of the many minefields spread along Kuwait's border with Saudi Arabia. This particular rescue took place during the early days of the Kuwaiti project.

The request came to our office at the Kuwait International Airport. The time of day was midmorning, about the middle of the workday. The request came from a crew working a section of the vast minefield. As information developed during the flight to the scene, we learned there was one patient on the ground. He was being attended to by one of the field medics who were specifically stationed at that site.

Immediately upon landing, I was presented with a patient with injuries I had never experienced treating. So intense was the severity of the injuries that even I was totally at a loss to know what to do for this patient. This person was one of three men working as a team to disarm anti-tank mines. The system for clearing mines involves utilizing three people in a team.

The first person works for approximately fifteen minutes finding and disarming mines. The second man, the observer, stands behind the first man and watches his procedures. The third man stays in a safe zone. Every fifteen minutes, the team swaps places: second to first, first to third, and third to second. This procedure ensures that the person working on the mines is relatively rested while he is handling the mines. The individual whose turn it is to actually disarm the mines has to bear the weight and heat of wearing special protective clothing. This equipment, which included a blast helmet with visor and a blast vest that extended down to the thighs, weighed about forty pounds.

Even with these precautions, it must be remembered that these munitions had been lying in the desert for over two years, and many were highly unstable. On this occasion, the mines were anti-tank mines. These mines have 2.2 kilograms of high explosives in them. They are designed to explode only when a weight heavy enough to crush the plastic top (approximately two hundred pounds) is applied. The force of the explosion is designed to have enough power to flip a twenty-ton tank.

To disarm the mine, you have to first remove it from the sand and flip it over. Next you have to remove the detonator that is screwed into the bottom of the mine, which is done by unscrewing it with a large flat-head screwdriver. This particular technician had a habit of using the handle of the screwdriver as a hammer to knock the sand out of the detonator screw slot. This technique had proved quick and effective for months. However, on this morning, the EOD technician's tried-and-true technique would ultimately prove fatal.

When the dust settled after the explosion, the place where the two men had been working had been turned into a smoking crater. The observer was thrown some distance. However, he was shielded from the majority of the blast by the working technician. The observer suffered a leg laceration, perforated eardrums, and flash burns. He would recover completely and, eventually, return to work in the minefields.

The worker handling the mine was not so lucky. After the echo of the explosion had died away and while the dust was settling, a faint cry for help came out of the minefield. This cry did not come from the site of the explosion. It came from a spot over forty yards away.

When the shocked EOD technicians approached the cries, they found the EOD technician who had been disarming the mine that exploded. He was conscious and crying for help. The EOD technicians and the medic on the scene did all they could for the injured worker. Now even before he was passed to me for transport, I could see the looks of horror in the eyes of the people who were carrying the litter basket. As he was placed in the helicopter, I could not believe my eyes.

The force of the blast had blown to bits every part of his body that was not covered by protective shielding. Both of his legs had been blown off at the tops of his thighs. Both of his arms had been blown off above the elbow, leaving only burnt bone ends sticking out below his elbows. The force of the explosion ripped off his protective helmet, shattering the face shield. These injuries caused the loss of one eye and an open head wound on that same side.

I had truly seen worse injuries in my career, but I had never had to deal with a patient in such a horrendous condition who was still conscious. The patient kept trying to sit up to see how bad his injuries were. I had no alternative but to hold him down so that he could not see what had become of him. He could now only see out of the one remaining eye, which was continuously filling with blood that was flowing from the hole in his head and from where his other eye used to be. All I could do during the flight to the hospital was to try to keep the blood from spilling into his remaining eye and to assure him that he would make it.

I prayed silently that he would lose consciousness. I did not know how much longer I could look him in the face and not let him see the horror that I was hiding. Mercifully, he died shortly after being rushed to surgery at the hospital. I had never felt as helpless and horrified in all my years and encounters as at that moment.

I don't do that kind of work any more. I don't miss it, although it is a part of me. I truly feel I have done my part. I have saved the lives of people that fate allowed me to. I carry the weight of the lives lost that I attempted to save; I am at peace with the conflicting graphic memories. I feel that I was allowed to intervene in the ultimate game of life and death.

Life will never again hold the same intensity as the heady days of life and death rescues. To continue without constantly living in the past requires peace of mind that the joys of the lives saved outweighs the baggage of the witnessed deaths.

ABOUT THE AUTHOR

Michael J. Disario has been happily married for thirty-seven years to a woman that he met and married in Germany. He has three grown children and is currently living in a little town in Upstate New York. He decided to raise his children here because of the family atmosphere of this town and, of course, of the 1000 Islands winter and summer sports. Since he has have lived up here, his house became a kind of B&B for family and friends visiting from the States and abroad.

Michael J. Disario was born in Saugus, Massachusetts. Michael's love of flying started at nine years old when he visited his grandfather in Florida. His grandfather was a pilot who flew in the Col. Ernie Moser Air Circus, St. Augustine, Florida.

He joined the Air Force right after high school and went to England for his first assignment at nineteen. While in England, he earned the emergency medical technician (EMT) and soaring licenses from the Royal Air Force.

After his tour with the Air Force, he entered into a contract working as a safety medic for an international construction company in Boston, Massachusetts.

Upon completion of the contract, he returned to the military by joining the army and advancing his skills in flight medicine.

CPSIA information can be obtained
at www.ICGtesting.com
Printed in the USA
BVHW021323051121
620551BV00025B/1098/J